EL DUQUE

The Story of Orlando Hernandez

EL DUQUE

The Story of Orlando Hernandez

Kenneth LaFreniere

Random House
New York

*Special thanks to those who have supported me always—
Heidi, my family, and the DP. Special thanks to Lisa Banim,
without whose help this book would not have been possible.
Also thanks to Jason Zamajtuk, Gretchen Schuler,
Georgia Morrissey, Artie Bennett, Christopher Shea,
Laura Goldin, Doby Daenger, Alice Alfonsi, and Kate Klimo.*

Photograph credits: Front cover: Allsport/Al Bello. Back cover: Allsport/Al Bello. Page 1: Ronald C. Modra. Top page 2: Associated Press AP/Marta Lavandier. Bottom page 2: Allsport/Ezra O. Shaw. Top page 3: Duomo/Chris Trotman. Bottom page 3: Sports Illustrated/Chuck Solomon. Top page 4: Major League Baseball Photos/Scott Wachter. Middle page 4: Duomo/Chris Trotman. Bottom page 4: Sports Illustrated/Chuck Solomon. Top page 5: Major League Baseball Photos. Bottom page 5: Major League Baseball Photos. Page 6: Daily News L.P. Photo. Top page 7: Daily News L.P. Photo. Bottom page 7: Duomo/Gregory Fiume. Top page 8: David S. Burns. Bottom page 8: Daily News L.P. Photo

www.randomhouse.com/kids

Library of Congress Cataloging-in-Publication Data
LaFreniere, Kenneth, 1975–
    El Duque: the story of Orlando Hernandez / by Kenneth LaFreniere.
    p. cm.   Summary: Presents a biography of the New York Yankees pitcher who defected from Cuba in a wooden fishing boat after achieving great success on the Cuban national team and earning the respected nickname "El Duque."
ISBN: 0-375-80197-9 (trade) — 0-375-90197-3 (lib. bdg.)
1. Hernandez, Orlando, 1969– —Juvenile literature. 2. Baseball players—Cuba—Biography—Juvenile literature. [1. Hernandez, Orlando, 1969–
2. Baseball players. 3. Cuban Americans—Biography. 4. Youth's writings.]
I. Title. II. Title: Story of Orlando Hernandez.
GV865.H458L34 1999   796.357'092—dc21   [B]   99-13618

Printed in the United States of America
10 9 8 7 6 5 4 3 2 1

To my mother,
the greatest Yankee fan I know

CONTENTS

INTRODUCTION

June 3, 1998
New York City

He stood on the pitcher's mound at Yankee Stadium as thousands of fans cheered his name.

"Du-que! Du-que! Du-que!"

Although he hadn't yet thrown his first pitch, Orlando "El Duque" Hernandez was already a star. Now, standing in the center of the most famous baseball stadium in the world, he took a moment to let it all soak in. He gazed around the crowd with an expression of disbelief. People he had never seen before were rooting for him because they knew he had risked his life in order to be there. And now it was clear that he had finally made it.

"Du-que! Du-que! Du-que!"

"Strike one!" yelled the umpire as El Duque delivered his first major league pitch. The crowd's cheers grew even louder.

"Strike two!" the umpire shouted.

El Duque took a deep breath and glanced around the stadium. Cuban flags dangled from the upper decks as fans stood on their feet, clapping and hollering for a strikeout.

El Duque began his trademark windup and...

"Strike three!" came the call from the umpire as the crowd went crazy once again.

El Duque had done it. He had pitched to his first major league batter and struck him out. He'd made it look so easy that it seemed as if he wasn't even trying. But the journey that brought El Duque to the major leagues was anything *but* easy.

In fact, it was probably one of the hardest journeys a person could ever take.

CHAPTER ONE

AT HOME IN CUBA

Orlando Hernandez was born in Cuba on October 11, 1969. Cuba is an island in the Caribbean Sea that is close to the Bahamas and Florida. The country has a population of eleven million people, most of whom speak Spanish. Cuba was discovered in 1492 by the same man who discovered America, Christopher Columbus. He called it "the most beautiful land human eyes have ever seen." It was on this island that young Orlando grew up and learned to play the sport he loved.

As a younger man, Orlando's father, Arnaldo Hernandez, was a great baseball player for Cuba's national team. His position was pitcher. Arnaldo was such a good player that he was given a nickname: *El Duque*. In Spanish, *El Duque* means "the duke." It is said that Arnaldo was given this title because of Duke Snider, a Hall of Fame outfielder who played for the Brooklyn Dodgers. The nickname fit Arnaldo perfectly. He was a very good pitcher who also had a great sense of style.

Orlando's mother, Maria Julia Pedroso, worked as a typist for the Cuban government. From the time he was a baby until he became a young man, Maria was there for Orlando with every step he took.

After Orlando was born, Maria and Arnaldo did not live together for very long. So Maria and Orlando, along with Orlando's older brother, Gerardo, lived with Maria's parents in a house outside Havana.

Havana is the capital city of Cuba. It is the largest Cuban city, with a population of over two million people. Although people in Havana enjoy their city, most of them are very poor.

As Orlando's family was also poor, the two-room house they lived in was extremely cramped. It has been said that until Orlando was sixteen years old, he didn't have a bed to sleep in. Instead, he slept on the floor of the room that his grandparents and brother also shared. Orlando's family had so little money that toys weren't even an option for him and his brother. In fact, many times it was a struggle just to have clothes to wear.

With his family's lack of money, times must have been tough on young Orlando. However, there were still many other things he could enjoy. Cuba is naturally beautiful, and the beaches that surround the island are considered some of the prettiest in the world. Many parts of Cuba's back country are also perfect for hiking and playing with friends.

The one thing Orlando enjoyed the most was baseball, the most popular sport in Cuba. Orlando has said that Cuban boys can be found playing baseball before they even start school. This means that Orlando must have begun playing when he was very young. However, because Cuba is a poor country, there aren't many fields to play on. There also aren't many bats and balls to play with. So many Cuban boys found clever ways to get around these obstacles. Any large open area could be used as a field. Four flat objects could be placed on the ground to be used as bases. Broomsticks became bats and a large cork could become a ball. And just like that, a baseball game could be played.

In 1975, Orlando's father had another son. He was born to a woman named Miriam Carreras and was called Livan. Although they had different mothers, Orlando now had another brother to play with.

Orlando and Livan did not live together while

they grew up. Orlando lived outside Havana while Livan lived on Isla de la Juventud, a beautiful island off the mainland of Cuba that was once a hideout for pirates and the inspiration for Robert Louis Stevenson's famous book *Treasure Island*.

Even though Orlando and Livan didn't live in the same house, they became very close. One of the reasons for that was their shared love for baseball.

As Orlando grew, so did his talent for baseball. At a very early age, it became obvious to everyone that he was one of the best players. When Livan was old enough to play, Orlando started to teach his younger brother the fundamentals of the game. Just like their father, both boys had a natural talent for pitching.

Pitching is one of the hardest things in baseball. A good pitcher must throw strikes, which means he needs to control where the ball will go. He must also be able to throw at different speeds. And if he can throw a variety of different pitches, he has a better chance of getting the batter out.

Although he was a natural, Orlando didn't just rely on his talent. Even when he was very young, he was always playing and practicing. Orlando's mother has said that all of the other neighborhood boys liked him, but sometimes they didn't like playing baseball with him because he was too good. Most of them couldn't hit his pitches!

On any given day in Havana, the people in Orlando's neighborhood must have seen him playing with his friends, and playing well. And with each new game, he had a chance to learn something that would enable his skills to grow.

Even from a very early age, it must have been clear that Orlando's talent for baseball would someday make him famous.

CHAPTER TWO

BECOMING THE DUKE

Cuba has a baseball league that is similar to the American major leagues. Different teams play against each other throughout an entire season. The two best teams then compete at the end of the season to determine a champion. Many Cubans go to the games to root for their home team. As a young boy, Orlando must have hoped that he would someday play for one of the great Cuban league teams.

The top players in the Cuban league are selected to play for the national team. The national team travels around the world to play in international tournaments, such as the World Championships and the Olympics. The government and citizens of Cuba consider baseball to be more than just a pastime. The sport is a source of national pride. Therefore, to be named a player on the national team is to become an instant celebrity in Cuba.

Because of Cuba's limited resources, its baseball facilities are not as good as those in North America. There are few gymnasiums where players can work out. So, many Cuban players take it upon themselves to find different ways to train. A player might find a heavy object, such as a block of cement, and lift it repeatedly to build his muscles. He might also run great distances to develop strength and stamina. As a young man, Orlando performed his own daily workouts in order to become a muscular ballplayer. As it turned out, his training habits paid off.

Orlando didn't have to wait long to start playing in the Cuban league. While he was still a teenager, he was already pitching for Havana's team, the Industriales. Not only was Orlando becoming a better pitcher, he also was developing a unique pitching style. Standing on the mound, Orlando would start his windup by quickly jerking his left leg up until his knee was next to his left ear. In the same motion, he brought his hands down around his right leg. It looked as if Orlando's upper body was curled into a ball while his lower body stood firm and balanced. Then, once his momentum was at full steam, he would uncurl and fire the pitch!

Because Orlando was such a good pitcher, other young Cuban players were beginning to try to throw just like him.

"Everybody imitated [him]," Livan said years later. "Everybody looked up to him that way. All my friends did. I did too."

Not only was Orlando's style unusual, but he also threw the ball from many different angles. A good pitcher must be comfortable with his release point, which is the exact place where he lets go of the ball. Many pitchers struggle to find one release point they feel comfortable with. But Orlando developed at least six release points he could throw from. Imagine that Orlando was standing in front of a big clock. He could throw from where it read 11:00, 10:30, 10:00, 9:30, 9:00, and 8:30!

As Orlando continued to develop his own style, it became even harder for players to hit his pitches. Imagine yourself standing in the batter's box, waiting for one of Orlando's pitches. You see him wind up with his knee against his ear. He's curled into a ball and you can't see his face. The ball is in his glove, which is partially hidden by his right leg. You don't know from which angle he'll release the ball and you have no idea what kind of pitch he's going to throw. All of a sudden, he uncurls and fires. The only thing you can count on is that it will probably be a strike, so you'd better swing. But, as many people in Cuba were finding out, the chances of hitting one of Orlando's pitches aren't very good!

In his first years as a pitcher for the Industriales, Orlando was already showing people that he was going to be a great pitcher. Perhaps he would become one of the greatest his country had ever seen. Fans constantly cheered for a strikeout whenever he was on the mound.

"Ponchalo, Orlando! Ponchalo!"

All over the island, people were talking about Orlando. "Have you seen Arnaldo's son?" they would say. "He's as good as his father!" The time seemed right for Arnaldo's nickname to be passed down.

Now Cuba had a new duke: Orlando "El Duque" Hernandez. The nickname would stay with him for good.

Although he had become a star, El Duque did not forget about his younger brother, Livan. Every chance he got, El Duque would help Livan learn the mechanics of pitching: how to pitch with runners on base, what kind of pitch to throw, how to confuse a batter. No matter how much he loved baseball, family always came first.

*   *   *

The life of a Cuban baseball player is very different from the life of a North American player. Although the best players in Cuba are considered national heroes, professional sports are outlawed. This means that players are not allowed to make money for playing their sport. They must work other jobs in order to feed and clothe their families. But the jobs that players have do not pay much money.

One of Duque's jobs was as a physical therapist in a psychiatric hospital. While he played on the Industriales, Duque split his time between working at the hospital and playing baseball.

Because it is extremely hard to live on small paychecks, many Cubans find ways to make extra money. For instance, some people sell ice cream out of their kitchens or use their homes as restaurants. Cubans who own cars might drive tourists around the island for a fee. However, if people are caught "moonlighting," or making extra money, they risk being fined by the government.

In North America, most players arrive at the ballpark in cars. Many of them buy very nice cars to drive. Most Cuban players, however, ride a bike or the public bus to the ballpark. Once they're inside, they never know whether the lights will stay on. In North America, players worry about a game being canceled because of rain. In Cuba, players worry whether a game will be canceled because the power has run out.

Soon after he began pitching in the Cuban league, Duque had impressed Cuban sports officials so much that they selected him to be a member of the national team. Now it was official: Duque was a celebrity! Not only was Cuba's national team cherished by its citizens, it was also the best team in the world. At almost every international competition during the past twenty years, the Cuban national team dominated. They were known as world-beaters because they would travel anywhere in the world and win. Now El Duque was a world-beater, too!

It was also around this time that Duque married a woman named Norma, a beautiful Cuban whom he had known for quite some time. After they were married, Norma gave birth to their first child, a girl named Yahumara. Duque must have felt like the proudest husband and father in Cuba. It seemed his life was becoming complete. He had a wife and a beautiful new daughter, and he was a player on the best team in the world.

Being on the national team had its privileges. Although his salary was still very small, the government gave Duque a house and a car and paid for almost all of his meals. He decided to use his new car to drive tourists around the island, which meant he had more money to give his family. He also had the opportunity to visit other countries when the national team traveled to international tournaments. Not only was Duque special as a member of the national team, he was also better able to provide for his family, which was the most important thing of all.

In 1992, for the first time in the history of the Olympic Games, baseball was played as a medal sport. The Cuban national team traveled to Spain to compete for the gold medal. Although Duque probably missed his family very much, he was very excited about the opportunity to win a gold medal.

As soon as the Cuban national team arrived in Spain, people from all over the world had them pegged as the favorite to win. "Cuba is in a class of their own. Nobody has ever really been close to them," said the U.S.A. coach. The U.S.A. basketball team was nicknamed "the Dream Team," but it seemed that Cuba had a dream team of its own!

In the fourth game of the Olympics, Duque pitched against the U.S.A. It was his first game in the Olympics, and he couldn't wait to get onto the field. Unfortunately for Duque, the Cuban team made three errors in the top of the first inning. Without much help from his team, Duque's innings were limited. However, despite their shaky beginning, the Cuban team came back to win the game by a score of 9–6. After this crucial victory, Cuba coasted to the gold medal round. In this last game, they clobbered Taiwan 11–0! After nine games, Cuba's record was a spotless 9–0. Duque and his teammates had won the first-ever Olympic gold medal in baseball!

When the national team returned to Cuba, the players received a triumphant welcome. People gathered in the streets to cheer and thank them for representing Cuba to the world. El Duque remembered these moments as some of the proudest he experienced as a Cuban baseball player. With a gold medal hanging around his neck, Duque was not only an Olympic champion, he was also a hero to all of his countrymen.

"Du-que! Du-que! Du-que!"

CHAPTER THREE

LIVAN DEFECTS

In 1994, Livan joined El Duque on the national team. It was the first time the two brothers had a chance to play together in international tournaments. It must have been a very happy time for Duque. He already had good friends on the team, but now he had family, too.

Duque had always wanted to do everything he could to help his younger brother become a great pitcher. Baseball was in their blood. So he continued to coach Livan whenever he had the chance. "Orlando has taught me everything I know," Livan has said.

Eventually, Livan became known around the island as *El Duquecito*, "the little duke." That must have made him extremely proud. Not only had he been given a nickname as a sign of affection, but it also compared him to his gold medal–winning older brother. Livan was quickly realizing what it felt like to be a celebrity.

In the 1994 World Championships, Duque led the national team to another world title. With his brother by his side, he went on to pitch spectacularly, blowing away the competition. It seemed as if no team in the world could stop the Hernandez brothers.

Although Livan was following in El Duque's footsteps toward fame, it appeared that he wasn't completely happy with his life in Cuba. He played for a great team and had a family and friends that meant the world to him. However, because he and his family were so poor, Livan couldn't do many of the things he wished he could.

With his small paycheck, Livan couldn't afford to buy a car. Instead, he rode an old bicycle wherever he went. Livan also couldn't afford to buy the clothing that he needed. He had only one shirt to wear when he played baseball. After each game, his mother would scrub that shirt by hand. Although most Cubans faced similar hardships, Livan had hoped for a better life for himself and his family.

Although many Cuban players love playing for their country, some of them would rather play elsewhere so they could make more money. Livan felt he was good enough to play in America, and he wanted the freedom that the country would offer. But could he leave his life in Cuba behind?

Under Cuban law, Livan could not leave the island to live in the United States. For many years, the two countries have not seen eye to eye on very important issues. The major difference between them is that America has a democratic government while Cuba has a communist government. As a result of these differences, the two countries have distanced themselves from each other as much as possible. A Cuban citizen cannot enter America without a special license or visa, and an American citizen cannot enter Cuba without a visa as well. Such visas are extremely difficult to obtain.

Cuban baseball players never receive licenses or visas to travel to America on their own. The Cuban government believes they might be tempted to try and play in the American major leagues and not return home. So if Livan decided to leave Cuba and play American baseball, he would have to do so illegally. A person who leaves his country illegally to live in another country is called a defector. The question Livan had to answer for himself was: Could he break the law?

A number of Cuban players had already defected, but Livan knew it was a very dangerous thing to attempt. If he was caught, he could go to jail for many years. On the other hand, if his defection was successful, he might not see his family or friends for a very long time—maybe even *forever*.

Unsure whether he should leave, Livan asked Duque if he would defect with him. He had always looked up to his older brother. He knew that if things got rough, Duque would be there to help.

But Duque told Livan no. His wife had just given birth to their second daughter, Steffi, and he was thrilled to have another beautiful daughter to cherish. He refused to leave his family behind.

In September 1995, El Duque and Livan were in Monterrey, Mexico, with the Cuban national team, practicing for upcoming international games. Both were looking forward to playing, but something seemed to be bothering Livan. Another time when he had gone to Mexico, he had bought a hundred dollars' worth of underwear. He sold that underwear for twice as much when he returned to Cuba, which meant more food and clothing for his family. This sort of trading was just one of the ways that Livan and other national team players made extra money during their travels. But Livan didn't seem to want to do this anymore.

Players from other countries didn't have to sell underwear. They didn't have to sneak down to the hotel laundry room at night to bring back free detergent for their mothers the way Livan and other Cuban players did. Thinking about this must have made Livan feel ashamed.

Livan again asked Duque if he would defect with him. Again, Duque said no.

One day during a practice in Mexico, a pretty girl walked onto the field and asked Livan for an autograph. Inside the autograph book was a note from a man named Joe Cubas. Cubas was a Cuban-American sports agent who lived in America. His job was to negotiate contracts for players so they could get the most money possible.

In Cuba, Joe Cubas was regarded in many different ways. Some people saw him as a traitor because he told players to defect and come to America for big money. Some people saw him as a man who offered Cuban players a better life. And others saw him as someone who was interested in Cuban players because they made him a lot of money.

Regardless of how people in Cuba felt about Joe Cubas, Livan was intrigued. Here he was in a foreign country with a pretty girl giving him a big-time sports agent's phone number. Livan became very interested in the possibilities.

At midnight that same night, Livan called Cubas's number. After their conversation was finished and Cubas had told Livan he could make millions of dollars in America playing baseball, Livan told Cubas to pick him up at his hotel.

Livan had decided to defect.

While his older brother slept in the same room, Livan gathered his bags and waited for the sports agent's car to arrive. Livan could have woken Duque up, but he decided against it. Maybe he thought Duque would convince him to stay. Or maybe saying good-bye to the older brother he had idolized his entire life would be too hard to do.

Later that night, El Duque woke up to go to the bathroom.

"Since he's my brother, I looked at his bed. I thought he was in the bathroom," he said. "But I checked for his bags, and they were gone."

So was Livan.

CHAPTER FOUR

BANNED!

The morning after Livan's defection, El Duque must have known that things were going to be very different. His little brother, whom he had spent years teaching and playing baseball with, was gone. The only thing Livan had left behind was a glove and a pair of spikes.

Duque felt empty inside without Livan. "Every day I was turning the corner again, looking for him," he said. "It exhausted me." One of the closest people in his life had gone away, and he didn't know whether he would ever see him again.

When El Duque and the national team returned to Cuba without Livan, some people started looking at El Duque in a different way. He was no longer the great Cuban pitcher who was teaching his little brother to be a great pitcher, too. He was now the great Cuban pitcher whose little brother had defected. In some Cubans' minds, Livan's act was unforgivable. He had abandoned his family, his friends, and his country.

Other people thought that Livan had defected so he could better provide for himself and his family, which was a noble thing to do. But no matter how his countrymen judged Livan's actions, some believed that Duque would follow in his younger brother's footsteps.

So did the Cuban government.

On December 7, 1995, Duque spoke to Livan for the first time since he defected. They talked about baseball and family. Livan promised to help Duque in any way he could. "He sent me a pair of training shoes so my feet and my toes don't bother me," Duque later said, laughing. "They're the best pair of training shoes I ever got in my life."

Shortly after their conversation, Livan signed a contract to play baseball with the Florida Marlins. His paycheck for signing the contract: $4,495,000 over four years. Livan had struck it rich! Now he could afford to send his family almost anything they needed. But there are strict rules about sending goods between Cuba and America. Certain things cannot be sent at all, and others are allowed only in specific amounts. If Livan wanted to send his family gifts that weren't allowed, he would have to find clever ways in which to do so.

After the news of Livan's big-money contract reached Cuba, the government became even more suspicious that Duque had plans to defect. But what they didn't apparently know was that Duque may have already had opportunities to leave Cuba. Since 1988, Duque had supposedly received many offers from agents like Joe Cubas to help him defect. But he refused each time.

"I'd rather have five million Cuban fans cheering me on than make five million dollars," El Duque said. He loved playing for the Industriales and the national team, and he loved his family and his country. Sure, they didn't have much money and sometimes struggled. But somehow they managed to find happiness in the struggle. He seemed content in Cuba. However, the government was still not convinced.

One day in August 1996, Duque was escorted from the practice field by two government officials. They took him to an interrogation room, where they questioned him for *twelve hours*.

The officials told Duque that they had placed a

man named Juan Ignacio Hernandez under arrest for "assisting illegal departure" out of Cuba. Juan Ignacio, they said, was known for helping Cuban baseball players defect to America. He was caught with phony passports and travel documents, and Cuban officials also found him carrying large amounts of clothes and money. Apparently, Livan had given Juan Ignacio the clothes and money to give to Duque. The Cuban officials felt that any contact between Juan Ignacio and Duque would be "dangerous."

The officials asked Duque if he had ever met Juan Ignacio. El Duque must have known that if he said yes, they would grow even more suspicious of him. But Duque *did* know Juan Ignacio. Livan had sent Duque clothing, food, and medicine from America. Juan Ignacio was the man who had brought him these items. Even though Duque must have known it would make his life harder if he admitted to knowing this man, he refused to lie. He told the officials yes, he had met Juan Ignacio.

Finally, the long interview ended.

Later that same weekend, El Duque pitched a game in Havana for the Industriales. As usual, the crowd went crazy. They chanted his name, blared on trumpets, and pounded on drums.

"Du-que, Du-que, Du-que!"

After the game was over, Duque's lifetime record in the Cuban league was 129 wins and only 47 losses. It was the best record of any Cuban pitcher ever. He had become one of the best pitchers his country had ever seen. Maybe even *the best*. But this was also the last time El Duque would ever pitch in Cuba again.

A few weeks later in Havana, Juan Ignacio was sentenced to fifteen years in prison. Within hours, Duque was ordered to report to Estadio Latinoamericano, a 55,000-seat arena where he had pitched some of his best games. He had no idea why he had to go.

To Duque's complete surprise and shock, government officials told him that he was off the national team. Only a few weeks remained until the 1996 Olympics in Atlanta, and the only reason they gave him why he wouldn't be traveling with the team was his "poor play."

Poor play? El Duque was stunned. After all, he was the most dominant pitcher in Cuba! He had the best record in the history of Cuban baseball and had racked up over 1,000 strikeouts. Earlier that year, he had won his fourth Cuban championship with the Industriales. He'd even struck out fifteen batters in his last game! In the 1992 Olympics, he had helped the national team win the gold, and he would probably do it again in the 1996 Olympics. It just didn't make sense to take him off the team.

Duque knew that the real reason he was kicked off the national team was because the government was afraid he would defect. Because the whole world would be watching the Olympics in Atlanta, the Cuban government probably did not want to risk an embarrassing defection for everyone to see.

Being on the national team would make it easier for a Cuban player to defect. When national team players travel to different countries, there aren't as many Cuban officials to watch over them. So a player can escape much more easily than in Cuba. That was how Livan had defected, and the Cuban government was determined not to let his brother do the same.

Duque must have been greatly looking forward to defending his gold medal in the 1996 Olympics. He knew how it felt to be an Olympic champion and he wanted to do it all over again. But now his opportunity to relive this dream was gone. He had very suddenly and unexpectedly been kicked off the best team in the world.

And even more disappointment was in store.

In late October, just before the start of the Cuban league season, Duque was ordered to hand in his Industriales uniform. He had played in the Cuban league for ten years and had worn his uniform proudly. But now the government told him his career in the Cuban league was over. No more baseball, *ever*.

El Duque knew that he had never planned to defect. He knew how much he loved living and playing in Cuba. Although he must have been devastated, Duque kept hope alive. He believed that he would one day be allowed to return to the pitching mound.

CHAPTER FIVE

LIFE AFTER BASEBALL

Even though El Duque wasn't allowed to play baseball, he continued to work out as hard as ever. He still woke up early every morning, ran approximately five miles, and stretched for thirty minutes. Duque refused to believe that he would never pitch again.

Although Duque did not let his spirit become broken, he couldn't help being upset. "It was very unfair because I wasn't planning to leave," he said. "I only talked to some Cubans from Miami who brought me some things Livan sent me."

Now that Duque wasn't playing baseball, the government had also stopped paying for his meals. He was also forced to move out of his home and into a much smaller house outside an airport. It was around this time that Duque and his wife split apart. They had known each other for years, but it seemed that the tough times had now come between them.

Although Duque was allowed to keep his job at the psychiatric hospital in Havana, his salary was cut to less than nine dollars *a month*. He had to walk to work because the government took his car away, which also meant he could no longer make extra money driving tourists around the island. With little income, and without the bonuses given to national team players, it was becoming very difficult for Duque to support himself and his daughters.

And he couldn't stop missing baseball.

"It's sad for me not to be able to compete," El Duque said. "What I do is go to all the games I can." But all he could do at those games was just watch. The only games he could actually play in were the ones that he and his friends organized in neighborhood parks. But even then, Duque wasn't allowed to pitch. If he had, none of his friends would have been able to hit the ball!

In a matter of weeks, Duque went from pitching in front of 55,000 cheering fans in a beautiful ballpark to playing shortstop in front of no one on a muddy sandlot.

And then things started to get even worse.

*   *   *

El Duque wasn't a hero anymore. The government had turned him into a marked man. As a result, many people in Cuba began to treat him as if he were a criminal. Police began harassing him on the street. They would yell at him and say things like "You used to be El Duque. But who are you now? You're nobody!" After a while, Duque refused to travel outside his neighborhood by himself. He was worried that the taunting might lead to something dangerous.

Amazingly, even though many people had abandoned him, Duque refused to be angry with them. "[They] have done so out of fear," he said.

Because the government believed Duque was a possible defector, many people were afraid to talk to or spend time with him. They feared the government might think they were possible defectors, too. None of the players on the national team visited Duque, because they could be banned from baseball as well. Duque must have felt very lonely, but he tried to remain as good-natured as possible.

Around this time, Duque met a young woman named Noris Bosch. She had first seen Duque when he pitched his last game in Havana, and she was immediately taken with him. She was a caring woman who wanted to help Duque in any way she could.

But even with Noris as a friend, Duque still seemed very upset. The country he loved so much was becoming closed off to him. He couldn't travel from town to town without the fear of being harassed. He wondered how he was going to support himself and his two daughters. He never knew if he was going to be allowed into a stadium, even just to watch a game.

And although he was one of the best, he couldn't take the mound.

El Duque and Livan were separated by only 140 miles, which is about two and a half hours by car. But now it seemed as if they were living in two completely different worlds. In America, Livan was pitching for the Florida Marlins and making millions of dollars. He had bought a luxury apartment on Miami Beach and had started to collect cars. In Cuba, El Duque was banned from baseball and making barely any money. He had moved into a smaller home and his car had been taken away. His situation had become so difficult that he was beginning to rely on Livan's gifts of money, food, and clothing.

If Livan hadn't defected, Duque would probably never have been banned from baseball. Still, Duque remained good-natured about his brother's decision to leave.

"None of this would have happened if Livan had not defected. But I don't blame him. He didn't mean to hurt me," Duque said. His world had all but crumbled around him, and it seemed it was because of Livan's defection. But Duque never blamed his little brother.

In fact, El Duque would often speak to Livan on the phone to give him advice about pitching in America. And sometimes, Duque would just congratulate his younger brother on his success.

In late October 1997, Livan reached the height of his success when he played in the sixth game of the World Series. His pitching was so dominant that it earned him MVP honors. The Marlins went on to beat the Cleveland Indians in seven games.

El Duque watched the World Series on TV. He saw his little brother holding the MVP trophy high above his head as his teammates clamored around him, cheering. The sight was so emotional for Duque that he bowed his head and began to cry.

"Crying cleans the soul," El Duque said later. As he watched Livan on the mound, Duque felt as if he were out there pitching, too. Because his brother had performed so well in front of so many people, Duque felt tremendous pride. "His victory is my victory," he said.

But although El Duque was extremely happy

for his little brother, there was also a part of him that wanted the same success for himself. He wanted to pitch in the World Series, too. If he defected to America, there was a chance it could happen. But he didn't want to leave his daughters behind.

When news of Livan's success reached Cuba, things seemed to get worse for Duque. Many times he thought he was being followed when he walked down the street. The police still harassed him relentlessly. Even his family was harassed. It was one thing for people to act cruelly toward him, but when they insulted his family members, Duque became enraged.

On December 15, 1997, El Duque's situation in Cuba became all too clear.

Pope John Paul II was visiting Cuba for the first time ever. The Cuban government knew that many media people would be on the island to report the event. They also knew that Duque would probably be interviewed about his banishment from baseball.

The government officials summoned Duque once again. They warned him that he'd better not cause controversy when asked about his banishment. If he did, they told him they would put so much surveillance on him that his existence "would be reduced to the size of a penny."

Basically, the officials wanted El Duque to act as if everything was fine, even though it wasn't. If he didn't, he would always be monitored wherever he went. The officials also told him that they had heard rumors of a boat being built to carry Duque out of Cuba. If this was true, they said, they would put Duque in jail for many years.

Duque's interview with the government made him realize something very clearly: No matter what happened, he would *never* play baseball in Cuba again.

CHAPTER SIX

THE ESCAPE

Duque now knew what he had to do.

He had to leave Cuba.

It was one thing for the government to take baseball away from him. But it was another thing to treat him as if he were a criminal when he hadn't done anything wrong. Everywhere he turned, he must have felt as if someone were watching each step he took.

Although Yahumara and Steffi meant the world to him and he couldn't imagine life without them, Duque felt he had no choice but to leave Cuba. Although he wished his daughters could be with him always, Duque knew he couldn't bring them on the very dangerous journey he was about to take. He could only hope and pray that he would soon be with them and the rest of his family again.

When Livan fled Cuba, he had left many people behind, not knowing whether he would ever see them again. But for the sixth game of the World Series, Livan's mother was allowed to enter America to watch him pitch. Maybe if Duque made it to America, was signed by a good major league team, made it to the World Series, and was selected to pitch in one of the games, his family would be able to come to America, too. But the chances of that happening were very slim.

December 25, 1997
Havana

It was Christmas night, and one of El Duque's close friends was getting married. Although his world had come crashing down around him, Duque seemed to be in very good spirits at his friend's party. He ate plates filled with pork chops, rice, and beans. He posed for pictures. He joked and laughed with friends. He and Noris danced to a song called "Ay Dios, Amparame!" which means "Oh God, Protect Me!" As it turned out, Duque needed a good deal of protection. That Christmas night, he and Noris had decided to defect.

The two of them made sure to eat as much as they could. Then, trying to appear as if everything were normal, they said their good-byes to the people at the party. Soon after, Duque received a call from his good friend Osmani Lorenzo.

"Are you in or out?" Osmani asked.

"I'm in," replied Duque. "Let's do it."

With that, the plan was in motion. At midnight, Duque, Noris, Osmani, and two other men, Alberto Hernandez and Joel Pedroso, piled into Osmani's beat-up red car and drove five hours through the night to a small coastal town called Caibarién. Alberto Hernandez, who was not related to Duque, had been a player for the Cuban national team. He had also been banned from baseball. He hoped to make it to America so he could play again. Joel Pedroso, Duque's cousin, was also hoping to play in America. Although they were all friends, not much was said during the long car ride. They were too nervous to speak. There they were, in the country they had spent their entire lives. Now they were riding through the dark night to leave that country behind, possibly forever.

At dawn, the group arrived in Caibarién and saw the vessel they hoped would bring them to freedom: a twenty-foot wooden fishing boat. It has been said that the boat had just four oars, a makeshift sail, and a compass made from household magnets.

Many Cubans had attempted to defect by boat before, but not all had made it. Some boats had been overtaken by the strong ocean waves and capsized, spilling the passengers into the water to either drown or be eaten by sharks. Duque and his friends had heard those stories. They knew they were taking the biggest gamble of their lives. It was very possible that they could make it to safety. But there was also a chance that they could die in the ocean.

Juan Carlos Romero had built the boat. He was a baseball fan and a friend of Duque's. He and his wife, Geidy, and a man named Leny Rivero had decided to join the group for the dangerous ride. In total, there were eight defectors. All they had between them for food and drink was four cans of Spam, bread, drinking water, and some brown sugar.

Imagine yourself in Caibarién, standing on the shore, looking at a small boat that's supposed to carry you and seven others across shark-infested waters. You have no idea if you'll ever come back to your country again. You're unsure if you'll ever see your family again. And you don't know if you'll even survive the trip you're about to take.

That's what El Duque must have been thinking that morning. It was probably one of the most difficult moments anyone could ever face.

Minutes after the boat took off, Duque picked up an oar and started rowing with all his strength. The arm that used to throw ninety-mile-per-hour fastballs was now paddling just to stay alive.

Although El Duque and his companions must have been very nervous, some reports have said that a speedboat was supposed to pick them up after they had traveled twelve miles. That way, although the boat was small, they wouldn't have to be in it for too long. However, the speedboat never came. The group continued the rest of the way in the small boat, no doubt praying for the sharks to stay away.

"The first part went perfectly. We made it out in eight or nine hours," Duque said. "Everything was going smoothly."

But then Mother Nature took over.

The calm sea started to get very rough. As the waves grew bigger, the boat began to fill with water. Noris became seasick and started vomiting. She seemed so ill that Duque was worried that she might not survive the trip. "There were moments when I wondered whether we would ever make it," Duque said. "But I had faith."

El Duque has always been a hero to
the children of Cuba.

In the Bahamas, El Duque takes a moment to celebrate his safe arrival.

Duque pitches in his first major league game.

Strike one!

El Duque is a big hit with the fans.

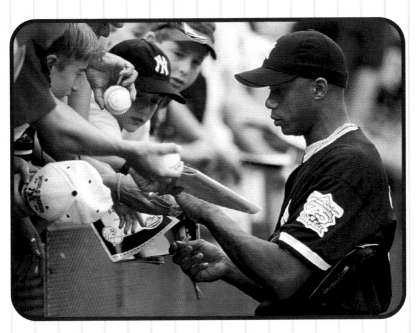

"Duque, over here!"

El Duque
focuses before
each pitch.

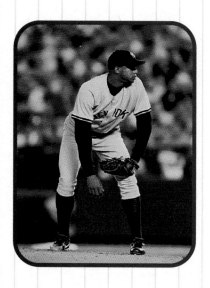

Which pitch will
he throw?

Hit it if you can!

When he's not playing, Duque spends time
on the phone with family and friends.

In America, Duque's thoughts are never
far from his family back in Cuba.

In the World Series, El Duque
used his unusual pitching style to perfection!

After the World Series, El Duque is congratulated by his teammates…

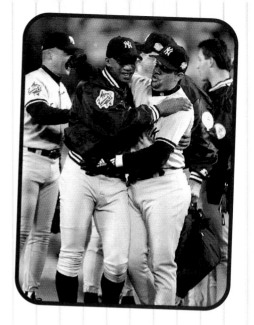

…and 3 million fans at the Yankee victory parade!

Duque meets his family upon their arrival from Cuba.

El Duque and his family, together again.

After about ten hours at sea, the boat was in need of docking. With only the makeshift compass to steer them, there was no certainty that the crew would find land quickly enough. In fact, there was no certainty that they would *ever* find land. Miraculously, however, they found a small stretch of shore where they could dock.

Although the group was relieved to be off the boat, they now had to worry whether they would ever be found. They had landed on a deserted island called Anguilla Cay. It is part of the Bahamas and stretches four miles across. Other boats from Cuba had washed up on Anguillan shores before. The crew found traces of these boats spread across the beach.

Immediately, Duque and the others went to work setting up shelter. The scraps left behind from the other boats turned out to be very helpful. The group used the wood to build a fire, and they also found an aluminum pitcher to cook in. Some of the crew hunted for shellfish that crawled on shore.

"We became like a family," Duque said. Each person had his or her own job to do, and they all relied on each other. They worked together as a team in order to survive.

For four days and nights, Duque and his companions remained stranded on the deserted island, hoping to be found. They slept side by side on the beach at night, using their body heat and the sail from the boat for warmth. All they had to eat was the leftover Spam and bread and whatever shellfish they could capture.

During the day, the group played baseball on the beach to pass the time. They used branches as bats, and they found old buoys to use as balls. Even though Duque was on a deserted island, unsure of whether he and his friends would ever be found, he still found a way to play the sport he loved.

On the fourth day, December 30, a U.S. Coast Guard helicopter flew near the island. Duque and the rest of the crew gathered on the beach, jumping, yelling, and waving at the helicopter. The pilot spotted them. A few hours later, the group was on a Coast Guard cutter headed for Nassau, the capital of the Bahamas.

After four long days and nights, Duque and his companions had finally been rescued. Freedom was waiting.

As soon as the news hit that Duque and his companions had been found, the media was sent into an uproar. *Cuba's greatest pitcher just defected!* Hordes of newspeople were immediately on their way to the Bahamas to cover the event.

The next afternoon, El Duque and his companions were interviewed at an immigration office in Nassau. Before the interview, Duque was reunited with his uncle Osilio Cruz. Osilio had left his home in Miami for the Bahamas as soon as he heard that his relatives, Duque and Joel, had defected. Their reunion was very emotional. Duque, Joel, and Osilio embraced in a crowded room filled with immigration officials and reporters. Their sobs of happiness could be heard over the clicking of the photographers' cameras.

"Thank God you've made it," said Duque's uncle.

"Yes, we have," Duque answered. "Forever."

But Duque may have spoken too soon.

Both the Bahamian and U.S. governments have an agreement with Cuba that says they will return all Cubans who leave the island illegally. And it appeared that Duque and the others had left illegally. This meant there was a chance that they could all be sent back to Cuba, even after they had risked their lives to leave.

Once the news of the group's arrival reached the Cuban community in Miami, a major effort was made to get as much news coverage as possible on the story. Joe Cubas, the agent who had helped Livan defect a year earlier, immediately went to work.

"I was working the phones all night, trying to make sure they didn't deport them [to Cuba]. We wanted to get the word out as quickly as possible and make sure it was out on all the news wires so [the Bahamians] couldn't act too quickly," Cubas later explained.

The strategy appeared successful. Once word of the group's escape hit the major news stations, American immigration officials granted Duque, Noris, and Alberto Hernandez visas to enter the United States. However, Duque refused to leave the Bahamas without the others.

"There is no reason to leave five people behind," Duque said of his friends. "We have to stay together. We're all going to be enjoying the same freedom together."

El Duque refused to enter the United States because five of his friends were not offered the same visas. He had risked his life for freedom, which he was so close to obtaining, but he would not take it until all of his companions were given it, too. Duque was indeed a great baseball player. But he was also a great friend.

According to Noris, Duque said he would rather go back to Cuba than leave without them. "For him, friendship is the most important thing. When he has a friend, he will stay with them until death divides them."

Because Duque refused to desert his companions—and with the help of Joe Cubas—all eight were finally offered visas to Costa Rica. Noris used her American visa and traveled directly to Miami to be reunited with relatives and to recover from the difficult journey. She left knowing that she would see Duque soon enough.

On January 7, thirteen days after they had left Cuban shores, Duque and his companions were off to Costa Rica, with freedom ringing in their ears.

CHAPTER SEVEN

ALMOST IN AMERICA

In Costa Rica, El Duque was very close to achieving his dream of playing professional baseball once again. But first he had to be declared a legal resident of Costa Rica and be given a passport. Once this was done, he would be allowed to try out in front of major league teams and show them how good a pitcher he was.

As it turned out, Duque was rewarded for his loyalty to his friends. By going to Costa Rica with them, instead of to America without them, he was free to negotiate a deal with any major league team he wanted. If he had gone directly to America, he would have been included in the baseball draft. That meant that he would have been assigned to a team rather than have his own choice of where to go. It also meant that Duque now had a better chance of receiving a larger salary. Because there would be more teams looking at him, he would be offered many different salaries. So now he could choose from the different salaries he was offered.

El Duque and his companions stayed in a hotel in San José, the capital of Costa Rica. When they went out to eat, they were mobbed by fans and reporters. "The owner of the restaurant had to shut the restaurant down because the camera crews and the reporters were driving them crazy," one person close to Duque said. In Costa Rica, people wanted to congratulate Duque when they ran into him on the street. He no longer had to worry about being harassed.

"In the short time I've been here, I've been enjoying democracy and freedom," he told reporters in Costa Rica. "Here, nobody can tell me what to say. It has changed my life already."

But when he was asked by a reporter about his family back in Cuba, Duque's happiness seemed to turn quickly to sorrow. "I didn't leave Cuba because I didn't want to be separated from my daughters, but the moment came to make a decision. It's difficult...I don't even want to talk about it." Although now Duque had freedom and would soon be pitching again, a part of him was missing without his family. No matter what great things were about to happen to him, Duque did not have Yahumara and Steffi and the rest of his family.

Now that he was free to play baseball once again, El Duque quickly went back to work on the pitcher's mound. For four hours each day, he practiced at the Antonio Escarre Stadium in San José. On February 9, Duque began to try out for major league teams.

Because Duque had been banned from baseball for a year and a half, many people expected him to be out of shape. People thought his fastball wouldn't be as strong, his reaction time wouldn't be as quick, and his stamina would be decreased. Not only had he not been training with a team, but he had just made an exhausting escape from Cuba.

However, Duque was in incredible shape. In fact, when one major league scout saw him, he said Duque was the most impressive-looking athlete he'd ever seen!

All of Duque's hard work had paid off. When he was banned back in Cuba, he could easily have given up. He could have stopped his morning exercises of running and stretching. He could have sat around his house in depression. In the whole year and a half that he couldn't play baseball, there could have been just *one* day when Duque said to himself, "Give it up, it's over." But he refused to believe it. Instead, he remained dedicated and practiced as hard as he could. Now that he was trying out for major league teams, his devotion showed.

Duque tried out for eighteen teams. But on March 7, the New York Yankees made Duque an offer he couldn't refuse. They offered him a contract for $6,600,000 over four years. Duque was absolutely thrilled.

"When I was a child, I followed the Yankees," he said. "They are the signature team of the major leagues. To play for them is a dream come true." Not only would Duque pitch for his favorite American team, but he would also become a millionaire. Back in Cuba, Duque had made less than nine dollars a month working in the psychiatric hospital. Now, as a New York Yankee, he would average $137,500 a month playing baseball!

Once he accepted the Yankees' offer, Duque's first thoughts must have been to send clothing and money back to his family in Cuba. Now Duque would be able to provide for his family better than he ever could before. He just wished he'd be able to see them again.

Luckily, he was given the next best thing. Now that he was a Yankee, he had to report to their spring training camp in Florida. But before he did, Duque planned to visit someone he hadn't seen in quite some time.

CHAPTER EIGHT

BECOMING A YANKEE

On March 17, 1998, El Duque's plane landed at Miami International Airport. Nearly three months after fleeing Cuba in a wooden boat, he had finally reached America. As he got off, hundreds of excited fans chanted his name. Noris came up and gave him a passionate hug. Duque signed every baseball the fans gave him. He had only been in America for a few minutes, and he was already being treated like a superstar!

That same day, Duque gave a press conference at a popular restaurant in Miami. Through an interpreter, he spoke of why he had to leave Cuba.

"The police would call my house and tell me that I was nobody and that I would never play baseball in Cuba again. Our families were receiving offenses on the street. They forced us to make this decision, which was very risky, but it was the right one for us. We are just looking for human rights, and we're in search of freedom. We want the liberty that God gave us to be treated like people. That's why we left."

In the middle of the interview, a buzz started in the back of the room. Behind the TV cameras, people were bustling with excitement. As the commotion grew louder, Duque looked up past the bright lights to see what was going on. Suddenly, Livan broke through the crowd! Duque jumped from his chair, and the brothers embraced in a big hug. Cameras flashed all around them.

Duque and Livan's reunion was very emotional. They hadn't seen each other for almost three years, ever since Livan had defected in Mexico. During that time, it must have been extremely hard for Duque and Livan not to be together. But they didn't have to worry about that anymore. As Livan kissed his older brother on the head, he told Duque, "Don't cry."

"Can't help it," Duque responded.

He was too happy to stop his tears.

When El Duque walked into the clubhouse at the Yankees' spring training facility in Tampa, Florida, he couldn't help but stare at all the food and equipment. "From the gloves and shoes piled up in the lockers to the food spread to the trainer's room, you could tell he was amazed," said one of the Yankee players.

El Duque agreed. "That's true...but the next thought I had was of the national team players in Cuba. I started thinking, why can't they have all that? They are also great players and great people. In Cuba, they give you one pair of spikes. You take what they give you, and that's that."

Now that Duque had seen the clubhouse and met his new teammates, it was time for him to take a physical. Each new player must undergo a checkup by the team's doctor so that he can be declared fit to play baseball. As Duque hadn't played in over a year and a half, some people wondered whether or not he would pass. But there was no need to worry. The Yankees' team doctor declared Duque the most fit athlete he had *ever* examined!

Finally, it was time for Duque to pitch. For several minutes, he threw to a Yankee catcher in front of the team and about a hundred fans. As Duque threw, it seemed as if everything else stopped. Everyone around, from the fans to the Yankee players, wanted to see the man they called "the Duke" pitch. The other Yankee players had heard of his dangerous escape from Cuba and already seemed to have a genuine respect for him. Now they wanted to see if he was as good a pitcher as they had heard. After Duque finished throwing, his teammates were impressed.

At the end of a fielding drill, Duque bounced around the infield picking up baseballs, even though that was the ball boys' job. He must have been so happy to be with the Yankees that he was helping out the team in any way he could. Not only did the players respect his bravery and talent, but they soon began to realize that El Duque was a good person as well. "I definitely think his attitude [is rubbing] off," said a Yankee catcher, Joe Girardi. "When you see how much he appreciates everything and you think about what he went through to get [here], it's inspiring."

El Duque had always dreamed of being a Yankee. He used to practice for Cuba's national team while wearing a Yankees shirt. Now here he was, living his dream. Things seemed too good to be true. However, one day during practice, one of Duque's new teammates asked him about his trip in the small boat and about his family back home. Immediately, Duque's usual smile disappeared. He looked down at the ground and replied very quietly. He didn't say much. No matter how well he was doing in America, Yahumara and Steffi were not there with him. He could never be completely happy until he had his daughters by his side.

After two quick games with the Yankees' minor league team in Tampa, Duque went to Ohio to play for the Yankees' Triple-A team, the Columbus Clippers. Triple-A baseball players are generally very good, but most of them need a bit more experience before making the big leagues. Some Triple-A players never do make it to the majors. El Duque was in Triple-A because he hadn't pitched in a while. Although he hadn't even played Triple-A ball yet, Duque knew it was only a matter of time until he reached the big leagues.

The Clippers play in Columbus, Ohio. Columbus is a city filled with large buildings, malls, and highways. It is very different from Havana. Whenever Duque had the chance, he took pictures and videos of all the places he traveled to in America. This way his family could see the things he saw, too. Everywhere he went, Duque always thought of his family.

Duque was immediately dominant in Triple-A. In his first game, he gave up only two hits and struck out ten batters. Imagine, his first big game in over a year and a half, and he completely overpowered the other team! He hadn't lost his touch!

Whenever El Duque pitched, more people

than usual went to the Triple-A games. Many of the fans were Cuban-Americans, who already knew of El Duque. For many of them, watching him pitch was a great experience. "He is an inspiration to every Cuban. To see him pitch in America is like living a dream. When I heard of his banishment, I was crushed. But now look at him! Here he is and he's wonderful!" one fan exclaimed.

During one game in May, a large group of Cuban-Americans came to the ballpark to watch Duque pitch. They could be heard screaming *"Ponchalo, El Duque! Ponchalo!"* just as fans had back in Cuba. After the game was over and Duque had won, a crowd gathered in the seats behind first base. Parents held up their children so they could see El Duque. Others held out baseballs and programs, hoping for an autograph. People called out to Duque, wishing him good luck in the majors.

Later, in the parking lot outside the stadium, the same fans set up drums in a circle and began to sing and dance. In the middle of the circle was El Duque, dancing and taking pictures to send home to Yahumara and Steffi.

CHAPTER NINE

NOW PITCHING: ORLANDO HERNANDEZ

After pitching seven games for the Clippers, El Duque's record was 6–0. He had pitched over forty-two innings and struck out fifty-nine batters. No matter how hard they tried, no team could beat him. Players walked back to the dugout shaking their heads, wondering if they would ever be able to hit one of Duque's pitches. They were also confused by Duque's unique pitching style. Few American players had ever seen a pitcher with such a deceptive motion. One moment, Duque was curled into a ball. In the next, the baseball flew past the batter for a strike. It was obvious that Duque was ready for the majors. The New York Yankees agreed.

On June 3, 1998, El Duque finally got his big chance. One of the Yankee pitchers had been bitten on the hand by his mother's dog. The cut was too deep for him to pitch. So the Yankees' manager, Joe Torre, called up Duque from Triple-A.

"It's time for the big leagues," Duque was told.

Torre told Duque that he would pitch just this one game and then go back to Triple-A. The Yankees already had several good pitchers, so there wasn't room for Duque on the team right now. But Torre had no idea what he was about to see.

When fans heard that El Duque would be starting his first game, there was instant excitement. Everyone wanted to see what "the Duke" could do. Was he as good as everyone said? Or was he going to be a bust? Regardless of which side fans took, Duque was cheered by the crowd waiting outside Yankee Stadium when he arrived.

"Go get 'em, El Duque!"

"You can do it, Duque!"

As Duque walked into the clubhouse, he didn't seem nervous at all. He'd been waiting years for this moment. Now that it was finally here, he was going to enjoy every second. He said hello to the Yankees and began focusing on the game.

In the bullpen, Duque finished warming up and walked across the field toward the pitcher's mound. There he was, with the lights shining down on him, in the most famous baseball stadium in the world.

"Now pitching for the Yankees, 'El Duque' Orlando Hernandez" came the call from the announcer. Instantly, thousands of fans were on their feet, clapping and cheering for one of the bravest people to ever wear a major league uniform.

Before throwing his first pitch, El Duque stood behind the mound and looked around the stadium. He would no doubt remember this moment for the rest of his life. The past difficult years—the banishment from baseball, the harassment on the street, the dangerous escape, and the uncertain rescue from the deserted island—all must have been distant memories. The only thing that mattered now was his first major league pitch. Armed with pride and his powerful right arm, El Duque went to work.

"Strike three! You're out!"

Amazing everyone watching the game, El Duque pitched seven incredible innings, struck out seven batters, and allowed only five hits. He got the victory and left the field to a standing ovation.

"I was shocked. I heard the Duke was good,

but I didn't think he'd be *this* good!" said one Yankee fan.

"He's bringing us to the World Series!" another Yankee fan cheered.

Joe Torre had planned to send Duque back to Triple-A once the game was over. But after Duque's awesome performance, Torre wanted to see him pitch again. So Duque stayed with the Yankees to pitch another game. If the first game hadn't just been beginner's luck, it looked as if the Yankees might have a new pitcher.

When El Duque was interviewed after his first major league game, he told reporters that he had dedicated his performance to his mother, his two daughters, and the rest of his family back in Cuba and Miami. No matter where he was or what he accomplished, it was clear that El Duque never forgot the people he loved.

His second game came on June 9, 1998, against the Montreal Expos. This would be an even bigger test—if he pitched a good game, he would stay with the Yankees. But if he didn't pitch well, it was back down to Triple-A.

Incredibly, Duque's second performance was even better than his first! He pitched all nine innings, struck out *nine* batters, allowed only *four* hits, and got the victory once again. By the time the game was over, people were in awe.

"He's like a Rembrandt…the guy is an artist. It was the best-pitched game I've seen this year," said one Yankee scout, a pitching expert. "I would turn to a scout sitting next to me and ask, 'Do you know what that pitch was?' And he would say, 'Your guess is as good as mine.'"

One of the best things a pitcher can do in a game is to confuse the batter. If the batter has no idea what kind of pitch is coming next, the pitcher has a better chance of getting him out. With Duque, the batters couldn't tell what kind of pitch he'd thrown even after they'd seen it. Was it a curve ball? A slider? Or was it a sinker? The batters had no idea. And if they couldn't figure out the pitch he'd already thrown, how could they possibly try to guess what was coming next? Batters seemed helpless against Duque.

After the game ended, Joe Torre sat on the bench with a very pleasant look of shock on his face. "We're going to have to see him again," he said. "We're going to have to work it out."

Now it was official. El Duque was a Yankee, and he was there to stay.

But after the game, Duque went back to the chair at his locker and sat down. He turned his back to his teammates, hung his head, and began to cry.

Nobody in the Yankee clubhouse was sure what to say. Duque had just pitched a great game and he was going to stay on the team. Why, then, did he seem so sad? No one knew for sure.

However, Jose Cardenal, the Yankees' first base coach, had an idea what the problem was. Jose was also from Cuba and had talked to Duque regularly. He quietly explained to Joe Torre and the rest of the team that Duque missed his daughters and wished they could be with him in America.

"It is very hard for him," Jose said. "He misses his family, and there is nothing he can do."

The only thing Duque *could* do was go out onto the field and continue making his family proud by the way he pitched. And that is exactly what he did.

Because he had pitched so well in his first two games, Duque was named one of the five starting pitchers for the Yankees. Now that he was a starter, people began to expect even greater things from him.

In New York, baseball players can feel a lot of pressure to do their best. Because there are so many newspapers, reporters, and fans there, a professional player may receive more attention in New York than he would in any other city. Could Duque handle the pressure of playing in New York?

"If the sharks didn't distract me," Duque said,

referring to the man-eaters that could have been swimming around his boat during his escape across the ocean, "nothing that can happen on a baseball field will."

July 4, 1998
Independence Day

"Today, for me, is a very big day," El Duque said. He was scheduled to pitch against the Baltimore Orioles, one of the Yankees' biggest rivals. But El Duque wasn't talking about baseball.

"Since December 26...I have my liberty. But also, today I'm celebrating my youngest daughter's birthday. She is three."

As he stood on the mound with his head bowed in respect as the national anthem played, Duque seemed to be a perfect symbol for the holiday. Americans celebrate the Fourth of July in honor of freedom. Who better to pitch on that special day than the man who had risked his life for that freedom?

El Duque went on to pitch spectacularly. He celebrated his daughter's birthday and the Fourth of July with another victory.

"I'm more confident with him than I am with a pitcher in his first year.…You look into his eyes and you see that he knows what he's doing," Joe Torre said about his incredible rookie.

"Every time there's someone in scoring position, he turns it up a notch. He finds a way to make a good pitch. He makes perfect pitches," said Jorge Posada, a Yankee catcher.

"He's invigorated me. Just watching how creative he is on the mound has rubbed off on me," said David Cone, the ace of the Yankees' pitching staff.

With every game Duque pitched, the praise continued to build. His new teammates knew of his bravery. They knew of his love for his family and country. They knew he was a good pitcher. But after watching him pitch his first major league games, they realized what everyone back in Cuba already knew: El Duque was actually a *great* pitcher.

CHAPTER TEN

EL DUQUE TAKES NEW YORK

Before he left Cuba, El Duque had run the risk of being harassed as he walked down the streets of Havana. Now, in New York City, he couldn't go to a restaurant without being cheered by crowds of people he had never met. In just six months, he had gone from a marked man in Cuba to a star in New York. And New Yorkers let Duque know just how much they admired him every chance they got.

When Duque went to the coffee shop where he bought his morning Danish, people stopped along the street and gazed inside to watch. As he walked along the sidewalk, fans called out his name. Cabdrivers honked their horns and shouted, *"You're the best, Duque!"* Duque had captured New York's heart.

Even though he had become a rich and famous baseball player, Duque didn't let his new status change him. "I'm the same person I always was," he said as he ironed his clothing in his hotel room. Even though he could now afford it, Duque didn't go to the glitzy New York clubs where many celebrities socialized. Instead, he preferred places where he could talk to working-class Latino people. And although he did buy a new car, he still rode the subway to Yankee Stadium, just like everyone else.

When he wasn't playing baseball, Duque spent a lot of time on the phone. Usually, he talked to Livan or his family back in Cuba.

On the field, El Duque always gave as much of himself as possible. When Joe Torre came to the pitcher's mound to take him out of a game, Duque never wanted to leave. "When you can't pitch with your arm, you have to pitch with your heart," Duque would say. He tried so hard for his team, and the Yankees and all their fans loved him for it.

His generous attitude showed itself off the field as well. Now that he was a millionaire, Duque didn't have to worry about how he would support his family anymore. Every chance he got, he sent gifts and envelopes filled with money to his family in Cuba.

As the season continued, it became clear that the Yankees were the best team in the majors. By the first day of August, their record stood at 76–27, which meant that out of every four games they played, they had won nearly three. They seemed all but unstoppable.

On August 13, against a very strong Texas Rangers team, El Duque pitched one of the best games ever by a Yankees rookie pitcher. In over eight innings, he gave up only two hits and struck out thirteen batters. He even struck out Juan Gonzalez, the American League MVP, three times! After his incredible performance, Duque walked into the dugout and was congratulated by his teammates. But before he could hit the showers, 53,835 fans wanted to congratulate him, too.

Cheering as loudly as they could, the fans at the jam-packed stadium rose to their feet and chanted for Duque to come back onto the field one last time. This "curtain call" is a way for the fans to say "thank you" to a player who has performed incredibly well.

As Duque walked back onto the field, the roar from the crowd was deafening. "It was the first time [the fans] called me out and made me feel like they wanted to see me again," he said later.

It was truly a special night.

Ten days later, the Yankees were facing the Rangers again and El Duque was pitching. This time the game was in Texas. Duque had pitched so well in the earlier game against the Rangers that many Yankees fans considered this one an easy win. Duque would shut them down, no problem, they thought. However, things didn't go as planned.

In just five innings, El Duque gave up eight hits and struck out only three batters. But even worse, he allowed seven runs to score—six of them in the first inning! The team he had pitched so well against ten days earlier had completely crushed him.

After that game, things started going downhill for the Yankees. Their starting pitchers were struggling. And for a team that relied on their pitchers as much as the Yankees did, this was dangerous. If they didn't keep throwing the way they had all year long, the whole season had a chance of going down the tubes. The Yankees lost four games in a row for the first time all season. Was it all slipping away from El Duque and the team that had seemed unbeatable?

On August 28, El Duque stepped up to the

mound against the Seattle Mariners. Even against hitting stars like Ken Griffey, Jr. and Alex Rodriguez, Duque pitched seven innings, allowed only three hits, and struck out eight batters. Against such a great hitting team, this was an awesome accomplishment.

From that point on, Duque's performances were practically flawless. He could do no wrong. For the rest of the regular season, whenever he pitched, the Yankees won. And, Duque's last three games of the regular season were some of the most impressive games he had pitched in his major league career.

Against Boston, on September 14, El Duque faced Pedro Martinez. The Red Sox and the Yankees were the top two teams in the American League and everyone expected to see a good showdown between Duque and Pedro. After the game was over, Duque had pitched all nine innings and had not given up a single run—a complete-game shutout. He had also struck out nine batters and pitched much better than Pedro, a pitcher known as one of the best in the majors! During the entire last inning of the game, the fans in Yankee Stadium stood and cheered for their hero.

"Du-que! Du-que! Du-que!"

On September 20, the Yankees played the

Baltimore Orioles. It just so happened that this game would be the first time in more than fifteen years that the Orioles' Cal Ripken, Jr. would not play. In 2,642 games, Cal had never missed a game, which was why his nickname was "the Iron Man." Because Cal wasn't playing, the Orioles wanted to go out and win the game for him. But Duque would not allow it. Pitching against a pumped-up Baltimore team, he allowed only five hits and one run as he led the Yankees on to beat the Orioles once again.

El Duque's last game of the regular season was against the Tampa Bay Devil Rays, the team he had faced in his first major league game. Again, he pitched superbly, allowing only four hits and one run as the Yankees went on to win again.

However, this was a special victory.

The Yankees already knew they were headed for the postseason, as their nearest competition, the Boston Red Sox, were way behind them in the standings. But after this win—number 112— the Yankees had set an American League record for most team wins. Not only was Duque a member of one of the best teams ever to play during the regular season, but he was also the player who had brought home the record-setting win. El Duque, the record-breaker!

Once the regular season was over, the Yankees' record was 114–48, one of the best finishes in the history of baseball. Duque's rookie record was 12–4, with 131 strikeouts and an earned run average (ERA) of 3.13. It was one of the best rookie records in the history of baseball. But although the Yankees and Duque had experienced an unbelievable season, they knew they had to win the World Series to be considered truly great.

Duque already had freedom. He already had the sport he loved back in his life. Now he wanted a World Series ring.

CHAPTER ELEVEN

THE ROAD TO THE WORLD SERIES

To become World Series champions, the Yankees would have to win three series of games. The first was the Division Series, in which they would have to win three of five games. The next series would be the American League Championship Series (ALCS), in which four of seven games would have to be won. Finally, in the World Series, the winner would also have to take four of seven games. If the 1998 Yankees could win it all, they would be considered one of the best teams in baseball history.

The Yankees played the Texas Rangers in the Division Series. The last time they faced the Rangers, El Duque had been hit for seven runs. Against great hitters like Juan Gonzalez and Ivan

Rodriguez, the Yankee pitchers would have their work cut out for them.

El Duque was scheduled to pitch the fourth game. However, he didn't get his chance. The Yankees were so dominant in the Division Series that they swept the Rangers in three games!

Next up were the Cleveland Indians in the ALCS. In the 1997 playoffs, the Indians had beaten the Yankees in the Division Series. No matter how good the Yankees were, the Indians knew they could be beaten.

After three games, it looked as if the Indians had figured right. The Yankees were down 2–1. With two more games left in Cleveland, the Indians had the home-field advantage. If the Yankees lost the fourth game, it would be nearly impossible to come back and win the series.

With the team's entire season riding on this one important game, El Duque was the man on the mound. He could either pitch a great game and keep the Yankees' hopes alive, or he could buckle under the pressure and the season would be all but over. If the Yankees lost this series, they would be remembered as a team that played well, but not when it counted. Their fate rested in El Duque's hands.

The last time El Duque had pitched in Cleveland, he had lost the game. He hadn't pitched poorly, but the Indians scored four runs, which was enough for the win. But the way the Yankees' offense was struggling in the ALCS, if El Duque gave up even one run, the Indians might still win. El Duque's game had to be as close to perfect as possible.

In the top of the first inning, the Yankees got a much-needed boost. Paul O'Neill hit a long home run to put the Yankees ahead 1–0. It was time for Duque to go to work.

Duque's first inning in the postseason was a very memorable one. At first, it looked as if it might be a disaster. After getting the first batter out, Duque gave up a single. Then, after striking out David Justice, he gave up a walk. With two men on and two outs, big Jim Thome came up to the plate.

The count went full—three balls and two strikes. Duque tried to throw a high fastball by Thome, but Thome got his bat around quickly and the ball went flying. The Cleveland fans stood up and cheered. They were sure that the ball was headed out of the park. Duque turned to see if it would be a home run. Paul O'Neill was standing on the warning track with his back up against the wall. He put his arm up and…

The ball landed safely in O'Neill's glove! A few more feet and it would have been gone.

Duque walked back to the dugout with a relieved smile on his face. He knew he had just dodged a bullet.

Through the next four innings, El Duque was unstoppable. He mixed up his pitches so well that the Indians had no idea what was coming. Although he was pitching in front of a hostile crowd, Duque remained unfazed. "I felt pressure, but no fear," he said. The fans could scream as loudly as they wanted. It wasn't going to bother Duque.

In the bottom of the sixth inning, the Yankees were ahead 3–0. Now Duque found himself in the exact same situation as the first inning: two men on, two outs, and Thome at the plate again. If Duque threw a bad pitch, there was a good chance Thome would tie the game. The crowd screamed for a home run. They yelled at Duque to throw a bad pitch. Duque wound back and fired.

"Strike three!" called the umpire.

El Duque pitched seven innings, allowed just three hits, and struck out six batters. The Yankees went on to win the game, 4–0, and Duque was named the Player of the Game. The fate of the Yankees' season had been put into his hands and he had risen to the challenge. The Yankees would live to play another day.

The next morning, El Duque was hailed as a hero in the New York newspapers. One headline read RESCUED! DUQUE SAVES THE DAY! Another printed EL DUQUE DOES IT! One paper simply said EL YEAH! Even the *New York Times* put a picture of Duque on its front page. Now people all over the world heard of Duque's triumph.

With Duque's performance in the fourth game giving them momentum, the Yankees won the next two games and went on to become the American League champs. They were going to the World Series! After the win, they headed into the clubhouse to celebrate. They hugged and congratulated one another, talked to reporters with huge smiles, and poured champagne all over the place.

Although his teammates were having a great time celebrating together, Duque sat by himself in the bathroom. He reflected on the last year of his life because it had gone by so quickly. In just ten months, he had gone from being a banned player in the country he loved to a soon-to-be World Series pitcher in a foreign land.

"I needed to have a moment alone," he said later. "I needed to think about what was happening. My mind raced back with thoughts of the past year. Although at times I've felt this was a dream, I am certain now that it is real."

When his teammates found him alone in the bathroom, they quickly included him in the celebration by spraying him with shaving cream. Duque laughed and joined the rest of his team.

Next up: the World Series!

CHAPTER TWELVE

BECOMING A CHAMP

Back in Cuba, El Duque's countrymen were ecstatic. He was a hero once again. "Now he's pitching for the team with the proudest history in the most famous stadium, and now he's in the World Series. Cuban people are very proud of him," said one Cuban-American radio broadcaster.

In Miami, "all the people were talking about was Duque this, Duque that," a close friend of Duque's said. "There is so much excitement in the air...El Duque is a hero." News of El Duque's triumph had spread all over the world. Whenever people mentioned baseball and the World Series, it seemed El Duque's name came up. "And what about El Duque? Isn't he amazing?" The rookie pitcher was a legend in the making.

But even though El Duque was headed to the

World Series, he still couldn't shake the sadness of not having his family with him. He hadn't seen them in almost ten months. Worse yet, he didn't know how much longer he would have to wait until he saw them again.

"Each time he pitches, he wishes for his family to be there," said Jose Cardenal. "He gets so emotional. He knows his daughters can hear the games on shortwave radio." If only his family could be there to celebrate his success with him. Then El Duque could be truly happy.

In the World Series, the Yankees would be playing against the best team in the National League, the San Diego Padres. Facing great hitters like Tony Gwynn and Greg Vaughn, the Yankees' pitchers had to be their very best. Joe Torre knew that Duque would be up to the challenge. He scheduled Duque to pitch the second game in Yankee Stadium. By moving him from fourth-game starter to second-game starter, Torre was showing that he had full confidence in El Duque.

"El Duque shows a terrific calm out there, no matter what the situation," the Yankees' manager said. "He has been that way all year and has always been there when we've needed him. There are times when you forget that he's just arrived and this is all still a strange place to him."

Torre couldn't have said it better. From the way Duque handled himself, it seemed as if he had been in the majors for years. But the truth was, he was still a rookie player in a foreign country. The confidence and strength Duque possessed were incredible. Luckily for the Yankees, he brought those traits with him to the mound—and to the World Series.

October 18, 1998
Yankee Stadium
The World Series

The stadium was packed with thousands of screaming fans. The seats shook as they clapped and stomped their feet. World Series ornaments hung from the upper decks. TV cameras were positioned all over the stadium. Millions of people around the world were tuned in to the game. There was so much energy in the stadium that the air seemed electric. Standing in the bullpen in the middle of it all was El Duque, calmly warming up.

"And pitching for the Yankees, 'El Duque' Orlando Hernandez," the announcer boomed. The reaction from the crowd was probably one of the loudest receptions that Duque had ever heard. He had come so far. Now he was finally here.

Now pitching in the World Series, Orlando Hernandez.

Duque quickly went to work and struck out the first batter. The crowd went wild. Then Tony Gwynn hit a single and Greg Vaughn walked. After El Duque got the next batter out, up came Wally Joyner.

With two on and two outs, Duque found himself in the same situation he had faced with Jim Thome and the Indians. Duque fired the pitch.

Crack!

The ball sped away from Joyner's bat as fast as lightning. The crowd at Yankee Stadium gasped. It looked as though it was headed out of the park. Again, Paul O'Neill ran back to the wall. He waited until the last second and jumped. He raised his arm and...

He caught the ball again! It was almost the same play as the one in Cleveland. If the ball had gone just two more feet, it would have been a home run. As he walked back to the dugout, Duque probably couldn't believe it had happened again.

In the bottom of the first inning, the Yankees did their best to give Duque an early lead and scored three runs. As it turned out, three runs would be all Duque needed.

In the next five innings, Duque allowed only

three hits and struck out five batters. Every time he recorded another strikeout, the fans cheered.

"Du-que! Du-que! Du-que!"

Duque coasted until the seventh inning. Then he found himself in a sudden jam. With one out, there were runners on first and third base. Luckily, Duque got the next batter to pop up to short left field. Next, Tony Gwynn walked. Then with two outs and the bases loaded, up came big Greg Vaughn.

In the first game of the World Series, Vaughn had hit two home runs. During the regular season, he had hit fifty. It was make-or-break time for Duque. With one bad pitch, the Padres could get right back in the game.

Once again, Duque refused to let the pressure get to him. Although he had never been to the World Series, he had already pitched in big games such as the World Championships and the Olympics. He could get the job done.

Vaughn popped up to the shortstop, Derek Jeter. The inning was over and the Padres' threat was gone. The Yankees went on to win the game, 9–3. Duque pitched seven strong innings, allowing six hits and one run with seven strikeouts.

After the game, the Yankees had nothing but glowing words for Duque.

"He was the same tonight as he was in

Cleveland," said Paul O'Neill. "He's a big-game pitcher. He loves the pressure. He's not intimidated at all. And he's fun to play behind."

"I love that guy, man," said Yankees second baseman Chuck Knoblauch. "For him to get to this country and have this success...that's tremendous."

El Duque may have even surprised himself by the amount of success he had in just a few short months. "I didn't think that I would be here today," he said. "But I did think of finding a way to one day be here." He had achieved what many pitchers in the majors never do: He had won a World Series game.

Although the Yankees had won the first two games, the series was far from over. Now they were headed to San Diego to play in the Padres' stadium. But Duque was still thinking about his family back in Cuba. Encouraged by one of his friends, he sent a letter to New York's archbishop, John Cardinal O'Connor, two days after winning the game. The archbishop had a good relationship with the president of Cuba, Fidel Castro.

Your eminence, Duque wrote, *I humbly ask you to use your good offices with Cuban government officials to allow my children to visit me.*

Touched by a father's plea to see his children, the archbishop immediately called Castro.

*   *   *

In Game Four of the World Series, the Yankees were in a very good position. They had won the first three games and needed just one more win to become the champs. It looked as if their place in history as one of the best teams ever would soon be a reality.

Duque sat with his teammates in the dugout in San Diego, ready to win the World Series. That night, it seemed, he and the Yankees would accomplish the ultimate baseball dream. But suddenly Duque was told he had a phone call waiting for him in the clubhouse.

It was a family emergency.

Duque immediately ran down the hallway to the clubhouse. *A family emergency?* Hundreds of thoughts must have been racing through his mind. *Please let everything be okay.*

Not only was everything okay—everything couldn't be better! The archbishop had convinced Castro to allow Duque's mother, his daughters, and his daughters' mother to come to America and celebrate the World Series Championship with him!

Duque couldn't believe it. He started jumping up and down with excitement, screaming, "They're coming! They're coming!"

*   *   *

As the last out of the World Series was recorded and the Yankees piled on top of one another as champions, El Duque cried with absolute joy. He was now a World Series champion, *and*, more importantly, he was going to be with his family once again. Right then, El Duque might very well have been the happiest person in the world.

CHAPTER THIRTEEN

THE PARADE

On the morning of October 23, about thirty hours after winning the World Series, Duque met his family's plane at Teterboro Airport in New Jersey. As Yahumara and Steffi ran into their father's arms, Duque began to weep. Finally, after thousands of phone calls and sleepless nights, he was reunited with his daughters.

"They and El Duque had a very emotional reunion," said a person close to the family. "Hugs and kisses all around. It was very moving."

When his mother, Maria, got off the plane, Duque held her tight, as the two cried tears of happiness in each other's arms. Duque's ex-wife, Norma, showered him with kisses. It was one of the happiest family reunions America had ever seen.

After the tears had subsided, Duque and his family rode in a limousine to his Manhattan hotel. Duque was laughing and singing and hugging his daughters during the entire ride. As incredible as their family reunion was, it was about to become even better.

On the same day that Duque's family arrived, New York City planned to celebrate the Yankees' victory with a ticker tape parade. All of the players and their families would stand on floats and be carried down the "Canyon of Heroes" on Broadway as fans cheered them along. Now that Duque's family was in New York, they could join the celebration, too!

Yahumara, Steffi, Maria, and Norma must have been very excited—and maybe a bit overwhelmed. After all, they had been in America for just a few hours. They had never flown on an airplane. They had never been to a big city like New York. And now they were going to be part of one of the biggest parades New York had ever seen, with over *three million* people expected to show up!

Riding on top of a decorated float, Duque and his family passed through the enormous crowd of cheering Yankee fans.

"Welcome to New York!" Duque's mother heard.

"Duque is the best!" a fan called to Norma.

"We love your daddy!" Yahumara and Steffi were told.

As they rode down the "Canyon of Heroes," Duque's family were treated like heroes, too. When Duque stood atop the float holding Yahumara and Steffi in his arms, tons of confetti cascaded down around them.

"I've never seen anything so beautiful," Duque's mother said. "I'm very proud of my son...still the same humble person he always was." Duque then raised his daughters above the cheering crowd as the fans serenaded the girls with the same affection they had given their father all season long.

"Du-que! Du-que! Du-que!"

Finally, Orlando Hernandez's dream was complete. He had his freedom. He had the admiration of millions of people. He had baseball, and he even had a World Series ring. Now he also had his beloved family back in his life.

Duque had won the greatest victory of all.